Mastermind Groups: Start & Succeed With Mastermind Groups

by Alex Genadinik

I0467518

ISBN:1519576897
ISBN-13: 978-1519576897

DEDICATION

Dedicated to my mother and grandmother who are the biggest entrepreneurs I know.

CONTENTS

1. 3 Free gifts for you
2. Additional resources that will help you with your events and overall business

FORWARD

The advice in this book is based on my own experience and success with mastermind groups and an interview I conducted with Alex Barker who is a mastermind group expert. Alex consistently runs a few mastermind groups at a time, and uses them to make money. In sharing the tips in this book, my hope is that you too will find success, and be able to grow your business or anything else using masterminds, or make money from organizing them directly. I wish you the best of luck in what you hope to accomplish, and hope that the ideas in this book can contribute to your success. Enjoy the book.

Before we start

A VERY WARM WELCOME TO YOU

Hello, I am excited that you got this book, and I want to extend a very warm welcome to you. In writing this book I did my best to cover every element that I think will help you get the most out of masterminds.

I hope you enjoy the book, and I hope to hear from you when you finish it. Whether you like the book or not, I'd love to hear your thoughts on how the book currently is, and how you think it can be improved. My email address is alex.genadinik@gmail.com and I look forward to hearing from you after you complete the book.

Why the book is so short: this is a relatively short book, but it is VERY to the point. My aim was to keep it short and sweet so that you can quickly get through it, not get bogged down reading things you don't need, and be able to quickly start implementing the strategies in the book.

GIFTS FOR YOU

As I mentioned, I am excited that you got the book and I want to make sure that you really get a lot of value.

At the end of the book there are 3 additional resources that I made free for you for free. There are also a number of very discounted resources listed there that might help you. The reason they are discounted and not free is that it just isn't possible for me to give everything away for free. But I did provide very big discounts to make it almost free. Browse all the resources there, and definitely take advantage of the free gifts from me.

While writing this book I debated whether to add the paid/discounted products. I realize that it might be off putting for you to be sold additional products. What I decided in the end is to only add paid products if they are REALLY helpful to you, and for a VERY discounted price whenever possible, while at the same time making sure that I give you lots of additional free resources.

CHAPTER 1: INTRODUCTION TO MASTERMINDS

"Whether you think you can, or you think you can't, you are right."

- Henry Ford

1. What are masterminds

If you are not familiar with what mastermind groups are, let me quickly explain it to you. A mastermind group is a group of people typically between 2-10 individuals who are interested in the same subject area, and meet on a regular basis in an online or offline environment to support one another, brainstorm solutions to challenges, hold one another accountable, and get feedback and advice from one another.

A mastermind group can focus on various business topics, hobby or general interest topics, or any other subject matter. Some of the most common mastermind groups tend to be for entrepreneurs who use the support and advice of the group to make faster progress with their businesses.

You can think of masterminds as small cousins of one-on-one coaching. One on one coaching is typically more expensive, so masterminds are great for people who need support, but are on a budget. A mastermind group member typically gets less attention than a coaching client, but they pay less. The advantage that masterminds typically have over coaching is that very often, the people in a mastermind forge strong business relationships that they maintain for years after the mastermind ends. And those business relationships can bring many additional benefits far beyond the immediate mastermind.

Another difference between coaching and being part of a mastermind is that a mastermind is typically made up of peers who are on approximately the same level as you are, and coaching is typically done by someone who is far more advanced, and coaches a person who is much less experienced.

Mastermind groups have their origins from Napoleon Hill who is one of the most well known business people and authors. He became well known in the 1920s. Napoleon studied some of the most successful people of his time, and noticed a pattern and a similarity among them. They all had what he called a mastermind. He defined a mastermind as a group of people who met together to brainstorm ideas, and together form a collective intelligence that is higher than the intelligence of any of the individuals taken separately.

Another trait of a mastermind that Napoleon Hill noticed is that each member of a mastermind was fully committed to helping the other members of the mastermind succeed. They were all invested in each other's success.

2. Why masterminds

When I was a younger and less experienced entrepreneur, I made many very bad and costly mistakes that could have been avoided with just a little bit of good advice. Instead, without that advice I ended up making mistakes that wasted many months of time and quite a bit of my money.

The power of coaching and mastermind groups is that it helps people who are just starting out in any field to shorten their learning curve, and help them succeed faster. That is an invaluable benefit that anyone could use, and is what makes good masterminds and good coaching so special.

Most young entrepreneurs don't seek out help, but seasoned entrepreneurs know just how much better their experience can be with proper coaching and peer brainstorming sessions. A good mastermind group can help you make long-term business connections that give you value for years to come, shorten your learning curve of whatever you are trying to learn, help you avoid mistakes, and help you succeed faster.

3. Ideal person to start a mastermind group

There are a few reasons to start a mastermind group.

If you want to learn something, and surround yourself with experts who are bigger than you are, you can try to start a group, and invite the experts into it for free. This will be like getting free access to advice of experts in whatever it is you are trying to learn.

Another reason to start a mastermind group is to have the support of people who are more on your level. These would be more like your peers who are going through the same kinds of challenges that you are.

Another reason to start a mastermind group is to make money from it. Many people would love to have the support of their peers, and help one another improve their standing in whatever field or industry they may be in, and to have a chance to have those people also become long-term business contacts. But who has the time to actually organize all of this? If you do, you can charge people to join your mastermind groups. You will learn something, build invaluable business relationships AND get paid for it.

Some people think that to start a mastermind group, you need strong expertise and clout in the subject matter on which your mastermind will focus. And in a large way, that is true. You can certainly have more demand and charge more money to have people join your mastermind if you are a well known person in the industry or subject matter that is the focus of the mastermind.

But it doesn't have to be that way. If you have no expertise and no reputation, you can charge a cheaper rate and have more basic masterminds that target beginners just like yourself. And other beginners will be willing to join your mastermind. As you grow in experience and notoriety, more people will join your next masterminds and you can focus on more advanced topics within some subject area.

4. Ideal person to join a mastermind group

Best candidates to join mastermind groups are people who are either starting out in some field, or are already actively working in some field, and want to see improvement in their achievements in that field.

The mastermind members have to really want to get the benefits of a mastermind because if they are not self-motivated and strongly driven, they might quit at some point of the mastermind, and make the experience worse for everyone else in the group.

CHAPTER 2: ORGANIZING MASTERMIND GROUPS

"Do what you can, with what you have, where you are."
                                                    - Theodore Roosevelt

1. How often do mastermind groups meet?

13

For most masterminds, not everyone can meet every week. Especially if your mastermind group meets in person, it is a lot to ask of each individual to allocate the time to travel back and fourth to a meeting location plus the time to actually meet each week.

If you host virtual masterminds, it is much easier to allocate the time to meet because you can do it from anywhere as long as you have your computer, and you only need to allocate an hour to an hour and a half to each meeting instead of a few hours that it would require if you had to get dressed, travel to a physical location, wait for everyone to gather because there is always someone late, meet, and travel back. With all of that, to meet in person can take 3-4 hours compared to conveniently doing a virtual mastermind meeting from home which at most would take an hour and a half with all of that time being productive meeting time.

Online masterminds can meet as often as once a week. The only caveat to that frequency is that it doesn't give enough time to try things that are discussed during the actual mastermind meetings and collect enough data to see whether those experiments were worthwhile. At the end of every mastermind it is a good common practice for each member to state what their goals are for the next time the mastermind meets, and sometimes one week is just not enough to accomplish much.

For my personal taste, I like masterminds that meet once a month or twice a month. This way it doesn't take up too much of my time, and there is enough time between the meetings to discuss new concrete issues and findings. But the meeting frequency generally depends on what works best for the mastermind members, the nature of the topics that are discussed, and how busy the mastermind members tend to be.

14

The meeting frequency can also depend on how many people are in the mastermind. If you have many members, each of whose issues must be discussed and given enough attention, you might want to increase the frequency of the mastermind meetings.

2. How to be a great mastermind organizer & increase the chances of participant success

To be a good mastermind organizer, your most important skill or trait should be that you are a good manager. You must follow up with everyone in your mastermind, make sure that people are on track, and can meet, and that the sessions run smoothly with everyone being left satisfied. You are also partially responsible to hold mastermind group members accountable to make sure that they stay on track.

A mastermind is only helpful to people if it holds people accountable to what they say they want to accomplish.

If as the organizer you organize the mastermind well, make each member feel accountable, and give them the tools and knowledge to succeed, it is up to them to actually follow through and do what they say they will do, and work hard. But you can encourage them and help them stay on track by following up with them outside of the mastermind meetings if you see that someone is struggling to do what they consistently say that they will do.

At the end of each meeting, each member should say what their goals are before the next meeting. As the facilitator, you must check whether each person actually does what they say they will do. If someone consistently doesn't accomplish their goals and does not even try to accomplish their goals, as the organizer, you must privately reach out to them to check what is stopping them from doing what they said they would, and either try to get them on track, or possibly let them out of the mastermind if they don't have the time or lost the motivation for it.

To help yourself with this as the mastermind facilitator, you can audio or video record your sessions so that you can pick out everyone's action items for the next meeting, and during the next mastermind meeting, make sure that they followed through on those action items.

3. How to run a single mastermind session

Each meeting lasts about 60-90 minutes with each meeting starting by having each member talk about what they accomplished since the previous mastermind meeting.

On average, a person can talk about their latest accomplishments from 5-10 minutes depending on the size of the mastermind group. If there are more members, each individual member can have less time to discuss their own business because everyone needs to be able to take a turn.

The point of this practice is to get each member to verbally say whether they accomplished their goals to everyone else in the group so that the group and ultimately they themselves can hold them accountable for what they said last time that they would try to accomplish.

The next part of each mastermind meeting is called the hot seat, and in most masterminds, this is where people get the most value from the masterminds. What happens during the hot seat is one of the members takes center stage, and the whole group spends 20-50 minutes focusing on the experiences, challenges and anything else that this particular member has to discuss at that particular time. Usually they share what is working well and what is not working too well. After listening to them, the other members try to offer opinions and advice to the mastermind member who has the hot seat to help him or her overcome their current challenges, roadblocks and struggles.

The group can also talk about the personal issues that prevent them from reaching success. These are often internal issues like lack of focus, low confidence and self doubt, not having enough time, personal and relationship problems, and a host of other psychological and environmental issues over which they can potentially get more control.

As you can see, a great mastermind helps to not only become better with a business or a particular skill, but it can also help you become a better self. You will have to open up to the group and often be exposed and criticized.

The last section of the mastermind session takes about 5-15 minutes where each member of the mastermind tells everyone else what they plan to do and accomplish before the next meeting. And essentially, the next meeting starts with each member having a turn and telling everyone else what they attempted to do and what they actually accomplished from their previous meeting's goals that they set for themselves.

As the mastermind facilitator, you can address each person during the start of each meeting and remind each person what they said they would accomplish during the last mastermind, and ask them whether they accomplished it, and what generally happened.

4. Opening up to strangers vs. people you know

There is an interesting psychological nuance that comes into play in masterminds. It is that many people who go through a mastermind notice how much easier it is to open up to seemingly complete strangers in your mastermind group vs. people who really know you well like your friends and family.

Even though your friends and family want the best for you, they usually can't relate to what you are going through. In most cases, they probably also don't have the industry expertise to be as helpful as the people who are in your mastermind.

Also, it is just easier to open up in front of people who you know are there for all the right reasons and who themselves will have to open up at some point during the mastermind just like you are doing.

Plus, if you are an entrepreneur, and if your friends or family ever found out about the kind of challenges, stress and hard work you are putting yourself through, most people's friends and family would think they the entrepreneur is crazy to put themselves through something like that.

Your friends and family would feel bad for you and would want to protect and shield you from what you are going through. But that wouldn't be helpful to you at all. So when it comes to your business or whatever your mastermind topic is about, the other members in your mastermind become like a small family who understand what you are going through in that particular time, and can identify and support you.

5. How many weeks or months should a mastermind go?

A standard mastermind that meets once a wek should be approximately a 3 month commitment. If you meet weekly, that is about 12 meetings.

If you meet once a month or twice a month you would need people to commit to 6 months or more.

Whatever you do, you must get people to commit to a set amount of time so that thy can pencil it into their schedules, and get used to regularly allocating time for the mastermind meetings.

There are some groups that go shorter or longer than they originally plan, but if you are the mastermind facilitator, you should get everyone to be on the same page in terms of the time commitment that they should expect. If they don't commit to a time, they will slowly trickle away.

Additionally, if you have a basic mastermind group which just focuses on getting people started, or accomplishing a specific thing like creating a website or a podcast or a YouTube channel or anything else, then a 3-6 month horizon is probably just right for most people to get started and find some initial growth.

But if you are a big picture thinker, you might have an ongoing mastermind with a few people who want to keep meeting (maybe not on a weekly basis for the rest of their lives) on a less frequent but still a regular basis, you can have an ongoing mastermind that lasts for a long time until people truly reach their bigger goals.

Of course, a mastermind must end sometime. So you can label your longer ongoing mastermind groups as 12-months masterminds, and the members can have an option to extend the mastermind out after reaching the 12 month mark.

6. How to find the right price for a mastermind group?

Charging and making money is one of the most exciting parts of organizing a mastermind group or any business for that matter. At least it should be exciting, but most first-time entrepreneurs sometimes have anxiety and self-doubt over actually charging money for something.

If you have a lot of self doubt about charging people to join your mastermind group, and you may be starting your first one, it isn't the worst thing in the world to make it free. Making your first mastermind group free will allow you to learn how to run one, and work out all the kinks before actually charging for your next mastermind group.

Eventually, if you keep organizing mastermind groups, if you are like most people, you will need to ultimately make money from it to make it worthwhile for you so that you can justify the time that you spend working on it.

When you are ready to begin charging money to people for joining your mastermind, try to think about how much your time is worth, and what you would feel comfortable getting paid.

On average, you will probably spend an hour and a half to three hours a week on a mastermind group. That includes the actual session times and some back and fourth emails during organization and call preparation. You should also account for how much time and effort you had put into the marketing, sales and initial setup of the mastermind.

Add up all the hours you will probably spend on the mastermind and choose a price per hour that you would like to get paid. If you divide that per how many people are in your mastermind, that should get you to your financial goal. You may want to overcharge a little bit to make up for any extra time you will inevitably have to spend at some point, refunds, or any other unforeseen issues that may come up.

Now you know how much to eventually charge to meet your financial goal for your mastermind group. Now let's talk about what is realistic when you first start charging any price that is higher than free.

For most groups that are organized by unknown mastermind facilitators who are just starting out, an average of $30-50 per month is very reasonable and affordable for most people. And ultimately, you don't want your mastermind to be free because if someone can't commit even $30-50 per month to get the benefits of your group, they likely also won't hold themselves accountable to doing what they say they will do for each meeting. They will just take the group for granted if they join for free.

After charging $30-50 per month, if you find that you are getting a healthy amount of demand from people who want to join your future masterminds and that the members of the current one are truly getting great value, you can regularly raise prices because it is always easier to go up in price than down.

7. Making the mastermind work for everyone's schedule

It isn't easy to have many busy people with different lives to be free all at the same time. People have emergencies, other commitments and a large number of other potential reasons why they can't make a predetermined time each week or month.

Some of the most free time slots that busy professional people have is Saturday mornings or weekend night time. You can also try to choose something like Monday night.

The next thing you want to do is actually get everyone to agree on the chosen time. The first thing you must do is make sure that people truly understand that they will need to be committing time to the mastermind. That means that they must be able to allocate some time on a regular basis to take part in the group meetings. You must emphasize that this time commitment is a prerequisite requirement to join the mastermind.

Once people all understand and agree to this, you can send them all a survey with possible regular times when the group might meet. You can give 3-5 times throughout the week when you as the organizer can make it.

After that, there is a little bit more of a conversation to get people to actually commit to some of the times you let them choose from. After you explain to them again that they must make the effort, most people typically agree on some regular time to meet like very early on Saturdays or late on some evenings so that they can clear other things off their schedule and be able to attend the group meetings.

8. What to do starting on day 1

A part of this book is based on an interview I did with Alex Barker who is a mastermind expert making significant money running his own mastermind groups. During the interview I asked him what he would do in my shoes if I wanted to start a mastermind.

Let me tell you a little bit about my background so that you would understand where Alex's answer came from. I am a pretty successful mobile app entrepreneur and an overall online entrepreneur. My areas of expertise are mobile apps, social media marketing, SEO marketing, online entrepreneurship, and making money from home.

Since I have my hands in so many different areas, I asked Alex how he would approach starting a mastermind group if he was in my shoes.

Alex Barker's answer was straight forward from the beginning. He suggested that for choosing a niche, you should not target people or demographics that do not have much money to spend. If your mastermind helps entrepreneurs or people who want to make money online, they typically don't have too much extra income to spend. So spend some extra time thinking about what mastermind topic might be in demand and at the same time draw people that do have an income.

For example, if you still want to target entrepreneurs, the segment of entrepreneurs that you do want to target are people who have a regular job, and dream of starting a business. They have a regular income, and are able to spend some of the money that they make at work in order to move their business forward.

The next thing to do is to start building an audience and either begin establishing some expertise, or begin making yourself stand out as an expert in your niche, and build an audience and a following by getting publicity, starting a podcast, starting a YouTube show, building significant traffic to your website, or doing something else that helps you establish yourself as an expert in your niche.

Once you are establishing yourself as an expert and growing a following and an audience, you want to begin teaching and explaining to your audience the power of coaching and masterminds. You want to truly emphasize the great benefits that masterminds can bring people, and how they can help people achieve their goals much faster.

After not too long of a time, many people in your fan or follower list will begin to buy into the concept of masterminds and begin to picture themselves getting the benefits of being in a mastermind group. And once they begin to imagine themselves getting those benefits and how much better their lives will be, they will do the rest of the sales job for you by convincing themselves that they need it.

After teaching and explaining the benefits of a mastermind group to your audience, all you have to do is offer people in your audience a way to join your mastermind group. After you have been teaching your audience about all the benefits of it, they might just flock to it. The only thing to truly make sure to accomplish is explain the benefits of masterminds to people really well, and truly make them see the benefits of it.

9. Four reasons masterminds fail

i. No risk involved and no skin in the game so people don't commit
ii. When there is no clear direction
iii. Lack of leadership
iv. Wrong people in the group

Now let's expand on these points. The first point addresses whether people take the risk by paying money to be a part of a mastermind group or not. Usually, if people pay money, they are serious about joining the mastermind group, and they will be more dependable. If, on the other hand, they don't pay to join, they are much less committed to the group and they won't necessarily value the group as much.

One of the great reasons you must make people pay is to weed out the people who are not really serious. There are many people who just sign up for many free things and never engage with those free things. Making people pay even a relatively affordable price will leave you with people who are serious, committed, and will value the group and the benefits that they will get out of it.

The second common reason masterminds fail is when they have no direction. You must choose a goal for the group, and some things that people should accomplish at the end of the mastermind. The goal should be as concrete as possible so that people know exactly what the direction of the group is, and what they should be able to achieve after the mastermind ends.

The third reason masterminds fail is when there is no clear leader in the group. If everyone is responsible for the organization of the group, such groups tend to lose track of people during the meetings, and from week to week the organization of the next meetings is full of chaos. That lack of organization usually spells pretty quick death for the mastermind group. There should be someone in charge of organizing it, and leading each meeting in a structured manner.

The fourth reason mastermind groups fail is that the people who join the group are the wrong people for the group. The people in the group should mesh well together and have good chemistry with one another. The people in the group should enjoy each other's company, and ultimately should enjoy meeting together.

10. How to host your mastermind with GoogleHangout

There are many tools you can use to host your mastermind groups. Some groups prefer phone-only communication and do the mastermind meetings on a conference call.

Other people prefer video-based tools like Skype or GoToMeeting. My recommendation is to use GoogleHangouts. GoogleHangouts are free, easy to set up and invite all the members through your YouTube account. There is almost no learning curve and they work well.

GoogleHangouts also get saved to your YouTube channel. You can share it afterwards with all the members if they want to go back over certain points. You can also go over the saved video if you want to check what each member committed to during the previous meeting.

Having your meetings with video helps you establish more of a connection and a relationship with everyone else in the group, and that helps to make your small mastermind community a more tightly-knit one.

11. How to get people to join your mastermind group

Marketing your mastermind groups is one of the most exciting and important parts of making money and ultimately being successful from masterminds. Marketing is never easy because it is always so competitive, but I'll try to make it as simple as I can for you here.

There are a two main high level strategies you can choose from to promote your masterminds. The first is to make yourself a prominent persona in your business niche, grow an audience, and then sell mastermind group entry to your audience. The second approach is to leverage other existing online communities in your niche to draw some of the people there into your mastermind. These communities can be existing industry forums, Facebook groups, LinkedIn groups, and by leveraging publicity on popular industry YouTube shows, blogs, and podcasts. Ultimately you should be able to take advantage of both of these high level strategies. If you don't have an existing big presence online at the moment, obviously the ladder strategy is probably where you will want to start.

As mentioned earlier, wherever and however you decide to promote your masterminds, you should always be talking about the benefits of joining mastermind groups, how much faster it helps people to fulfill their goals, and how much easier and more enjoyable their experience will become. As you keep talking about the benefits of joining mastermind groups, many people will take a strong interest in masterminds and as you keep talking about and promoting your mastermind groups, their interest will build and naturally develop into desire, and they will join your groups.

Posting in relevant communities is relatively simple as long as you get to know the rules of the communities in which you post, and don't post there in an overly promotional way, and make sure with the admins of those groups that it is OK to post whatever you are about to post.

As far as building your own audience, that is much more difficult. It is a better long-term strategy because if you grow a big audience with a big blog, podcast, YouTube show, or anything else, you will get many new potential clients discovering your work every single day. It will be like generating daily publicity for your business. Plus, by the time you will want to promote your mastermind group, those people will already be very familiar with your work, and trust that you will give them value.

The challenge is that it takes time to build an audience, and a lot of work to build a prominent podcast or a YouTube channel or a blog.

Building tremendous traffic or a successful podcast or YouTube show is obviously a lot of work and is extremely difficult, and can't really be covered in this book fully. But the good news is that I teach many elements of it in my online courses. And as one of my gifts to you that I mentioned earlier in this book, you can have free access to one of the online courses to help you get started with whatever approach you are interested in pursuing. Here is my full list of courses that you can browse and choose one for free:

https://www.udemy.com/user/alexgenadinik

Later in the book I explain how to easily get it for free along with additional free and very discounted resources.

Another thing you can do to get people into your mastermind is to email or contact them via other means individually. I realize that this sounds like a pain, and it might be, but if you hand select people, and write them personal emails with reasons why they should join, they will be much more likely to join.

I had this happen to me. Someone emailed me once saying that they were just starting out in some online niche in which I was already somewhat prominent in, but was trying to grow and was facing a number of challenges. At first I was skeptical because I thought that I couldn't learn anything from that person since they were just starting out.

To convince me they mentioned a few of the other big names in that niche, and said that they were trying to also invite those people into the mastermind. Those big names got me excited because I wanted to learn from them, and it got me to agree to join that particular mastermind. I ended up getting quite a bit of benefit from that mastermind, and that happened because the person who invited me sent me a personal invitation, and sold it to me using social proof that he himself didn't have, but that potential other members in the group did have.

In my interview with Alex Barker, he recommended that as the organizer of the mastermind, when you are trying to get people into it, it is important to get them on the phone so that you can convince them to join, and also vet them a little bit to make sure that they are not the wrong people for your mastermind group. Once you perfect your sales pitch, getting on the phone with people can increase your sales conversion rate, and help you get more quality people to join your mastermind.

You can also give people incentives to recommend their friends to join your mastermind by paying them a commission. You should establish many contacts in your business niche, and make it known that you want to offer a commission for a referral that converts into a client. This way you will get other people referring you good potential leads.

12. How much money you can make from masterminds

If you charge just $50/month per person, and have 7 people in your mastermind group, that will be $350 per month per mastermind group.

If you spend an average of 2 hours per week on running the mastermind, that would equate to somewhere between 8-10 hours per month of work. Let's say that you spend 10 hours per month on a mastermind. If you do, that would equate to a salary of $35 per hour working from home on your own time (in your shorts).

That is pretty decent for most people, and as a full time job this can earn you a middle class salary in United States.

If you spend 40 hours per week on your mastermind business, you can earn $1,400 each week, and $5,600 every 4 weeks.

Of course, it isn't that easy to have so many mastermind groups run concurrently due to scheduling issues since there are only a few ideal times during the week for a mastermind to meet. Nevertheless, you can work up to it over time as you hit your groove in organizing masterminds.

You can also raise the mastermind prices once you hit very high demand so that you won't have to work so much, and still make a very reasonable salary. Imagine if you charged $100 per month to join your mastermind instead of $50. This would make you about $12,000 each month, which is a very good salary of $144,000 per year.

Now let's come down from the clouds. It isn't easy to get to that level, and when you first start, it will be a struggle. You just have to begin with running one or two mastermind groups at a time, becoming a good mastermind organizer, and get better and better at promoting your mastermind and helping people get results from them. Over time you can add more time slots during which you run new masterminds, and add additional industries or niches that your masterminds cover.

Ultimately, with anything you do, the sky is the limit. But in the beginning, you must walk before you can run, and run before you can fly.

13. Additional revenue streams for masterminds

There are additional ways to make money from your mastermind groups.

Obviously the main way to make money from masterminds is by charging people directly for joining the groups, but like in any business, you must find ways to maximize the lifetime earnings you get from each client, and hopefully make them long-term clients.

There is a common understanding in business that in most cases, it is easier to sell something to an existing client than to find a new client.

One immediate thing you can do when a mastermind group is over is to invite people to further mastermind groups, or to extend the current mastermind groups. This can immediately increase your revenue.

Another thing you can do is to create digital products like online courses or books or something else, and make that available to the members of your masterminds. Of course, these products have to be within the same niche that your particular masterminds cover so that they are compelling products for your group members. Having extra products to sell can maximize your revenue and ultimate profit per customer.

You can also up-sell one-on-one coaching to people who are extra passionate and engaged members of your masterminds.

To up-sell people and get them to join additional mastermind groups or coaching, towards the end of the mastermind group, you can call your group members and ask them about what value they feel that they have gotten from your mastermind. After that, as they talk about how beneficial the mastermind was for them, you can invite them into additional masterminds since at that point they have talked up all the benefits they have gotten from your masterminds, and are emotionally feeling very positive about it.

You can also ask those people who they might know who also struggles with the things that the mastermind helps people with. This way your existing mastermind group members can help you generate leads that might turn into clients.

14. Long term value of creating masterminds

It may not be immediately apparent when you join a mastermind group, but the people with whom you are in a mastermind are very likely to become long-term business contacts with whom you might develop great business relationships for years to come.

A single great long-term business relationship can bring both of the people in it benefits and even decades to come. As both of you grow in your careers, you will also be able to give each other bigger and better benefits.

Now imagine if you regularly organize and run mastermind groups. You will have many such very strong business relationships relatively quickly, and hundreds over the span of your career.

Now imagine what happens when you launch some book or some product or have anything else to promote, announce, or get other kinds of help with. You can then reach out to all those people and have them share your launch or any other big announcement to their audiences, and create an army of people who are promoting your launch or any other big announcement for you, or helping you in whatever other things you need help with.

Having so many quality business contacts gives you immense power moving forward for the rest of your career.

The End

Best of luck starting your own masterminds and joining the masterminds of others! I wish you amazing success in everything you do, and really hope that the strategies in this book bring you more success in whatever you are trying to accomplish, and more quality and long-term business relationships.

WHAT DID YOU THINK OF THIS BOOK?

I want to hear from you. If you liked the book or didn't, please email me your thoughts to my email
alex.genadinik@gmail.com

FURTHER FREE RESOURCES AND DISCOUNTS

FREE GIFTS FOR YOU AND EXTRA RESOURCES

Gift 1: I will give you one free online business/marketing course of YOUR choosing and huge discounts on any additional courses.

I teach over 60 online courses on business and marketing. Just for you, I will give you one for absolutely free, and you choose which one. Browse my full list of courses and email me telling me which course you want, and I will send you a free coupon!

Here is my full list of courses:

https://www.udemy.com/user/alexgenadinik/

Just send me an email to alex.genadinik@gmail.com and tell me that you got this book, and which of my courses you would like for free, and I will send you a coupon code to get that course for free.

Want any additional courses? To get any other course for almost free, use the discount coupon code: thankyouforreading

Gift: 2: Get my Android business apps for free.

My apps come as a 4-app course and on Android I have free versions of each!

Free business plan app:
https://play.google.com/store/apps/details?id=com.problemio&hl=en

Free marketing app:
https://play.google.com/store/apps/details?id=com.marketing&hl=en

Free app on fundraising and making money:
https://play.google.com/store/apps/details?id=make.money&hl=en

Free business idea app:

https://play.google.com/store/apps/details?id=business.ideas&hl=en

I am sorry, but my iPhone apps are not free and it isn't easy to make them free. But if you are interested, they start at just $0.99 and you can browse all my paid apps on my website: http://www.problemio.com

Gift 3: **Free business advice**

If you have questions about your events, your overall business, or anything mentioned in this book, email me at alex.genadinik@gmail.com and I will be happy to help you. Just please keep two things in mind:

1) Remind me that you got this book and that you are not just a random person on the Internet.
2) Please make the questions clear and short. I love to help, but I am often overwhelmed with work, and always short on the time that I have available.

COMPLETE LIST OF MY BOOKS

If you enjoyed this book, check out my Amazon author page to see the full list of my books:
http://www.amazon.com/Alex-Genadinik/e/B00I114WEU

VERY AFFORDABLE BUSINESS COACHING FROM ME

Here is a way you can get really affordable business and marketing coaching from me, in a one on one Skype call where you and I discuss everything about your business. I know this gig talks about SEO strategy, but we can talk about anything you want regarding your business. The key is that you and I get on a Skype call with the gig that you buy with this link:

https://www.fiverr.com/genadinik/help-you-plan-an-seo-strategy

DID YOU ENJOY THE BOOK?

If you liked the book, I would sincerely appreciate it if you left a review about your experience on Amazon.

And if you didn't enjoy it, or were expecting to get different things out of it, please email me at alex.genadinik@gmail.com and I will be happy to add/edit material in this book to make it better.

Thank you for reading and please keep in touch!

ABOUT THE AUTHOR

Alex Genadinik is a software engineer, an entrepreneur, and a marketer. Alex is a 3-time best selling Amazon author, and the creator of the Problemio.com business apps which are some of the top mobile apps for planning and starting a business with 1,000,000 downloads across iOS, Android and Kindle. Alex has a B.S in Computer Science from San Jose State University.

Alex is also a prominent online teacher, and loves to help entrepreneurs achieve their dreams.

www.ingramcontent.com/pod-product-compliance
Lightning Source LLC
Chambersburg PA
CBHW051225170526
45166CB00005B/2054